Reasons for Naturalizing the Jews in Great Britain and Ireland,
On the same foot with all other nations.
Containing also, A Defence of the Jews against All vulgar Prejudices in all Countries.

John Toland (1670-1722)

Have we not all one father? Has not one God created us? Why do we deal treacherously every one with his neighbour? Mal I. 10.

Uttnam qui ubique sunt Propugnatores hujus Imperii, possent in hanc Civitatem venire, & contra Oppugnatores Respublicae de Civitate exterminum. Cic. in Orat. pro L. Corn Balbo. cap. 2.

TMP
Publications

Original author, John Toland (1670-1722). First published in 1714.

This edition published by The Manuscript Publisher, 2013

General Editor: J.N. Duggan

ISBN: 978-0-9571157-8-1

A CIP Catalogue record for this book is available from the British Library

Digitisation, typesetting and cover design by DocumentsandManuscripts.com

Cover image illustrations include *Robert Modern's Map of England, Scotland and Ireland c. 1680,* the only known image of John Toland (1670-1722) and *Nautical chart of Mediterranean area, including Europe with British Isles and part of Scandinavia, c. 1600.* Source: Wikimedia Commons.
Star of David and Menorah (Hanukkah) symbols reproduced from OpenClipArt.org

Publishing solutions for the digital age. For more information please visit: www.TheManuscriptPublisher.com

The only known image of John Toland (1670-1722)

Contents

Introduction

John Toland was born in Donegal, Ireland to a Gaelic-speaking Catholic family on November 30th 1670. At the age of sixteen he joined the Church of Ireland which enabled him to receive an education at the Protestant school of Redcastle. He attended the University of Glasgow, where he gained a scholarship to study theology and later graduated with a Master of Arts from Edinburgh University in 1690 - the day before the Battle of the Boyne as he recalled. He also attended the University of Leyden and then returned to England, where he stayed in prominent Whig households in Oxford and London, earning his living as a propagandist for the Whig party.

In 1696 he published Christianity not Mysterious, which argued that anything in Christianity that appeared to be contrary to reason was simply due to mistranslations from the original gospels, additions by the clergy which increased their own authority, or misunderstandings on the part of the Fathers and Doctors of the Church. The book was published in London where it caused a minor stir, but in Dublin it was banned and burnt, and Toland fled his native country, never to return.

He travelled widely on the continent, studying ancient manuscripts and constantly adding to his store of languages and knowledge of other religions, but always bringing an independent mind to everything he read and saw. He was the first man to be called a 'Free Thinker' and he well deserved the name; never accepting anything at face value, but always bringing his own knowledge and judgement to bear on any subject.

In 1701 he travelled with the British Delegation to Hanover to deliver a copy of the Act of Settlement to Sophia of Hanover, who was named in it as Heiress of Great Britain. Both Sophia and her daughter Sophie

Charlotte, Queen in Prussia enjoyed his company and he became strongly attached to the House of Hanover, despite his Republican leanings.

He was a prolific writer and pamphleteer, writing on an enormous variety of subjects: politics, religion, banks, history, literature, philosophy. etc. He wrote this essay in 1714, months after the succession of George I to the British throne.

In 1709 the Act of Naturalisation for Foreign Protestants had been passed by the British Parliament, which allowed foreign Protestant immigrants to claim British citizenship upon swearing an oath of allegiance to the British throne and taking the sacrament in a Protestant church. It was as a result of this Act that some 13,000 Palatines from the Rhine Palatinate emigrated to England, Ireland and the American Colonies. Toland is calling in this pamphlet for the same privileges to be extended to the Jews.

Editor's Note

John Toland wrote this pamphlet in December 1714, four months after the Accession of George I to the throne of Great Britain on August 1st 1714.

The Acts that he refers to are:

(1) The Act of Naturalization of the Most Excellent Princess Sophia, Electress and Duchess Dowager of Hanover and the issue of her body, if Protestant, which conferred British citizenship on Sophia and her descendants (as long as they were legitimate and Protestant). This Act was not repealed until 1948.

(2) The Foreign and Protestants Naturalization Act 1709 which gave British citizenship to Protestant immigrants from France and from The Palatinate in Germany, for the very modest sum of one shilling and the swearing of certain oaths. This was a Whig bill and the Tories repealed it when they came to power in 1712, but the repeal was not retroactive and anyone who had already claimed citizenship was allowed to retain it.

REASONS

FOR

NATURALIZING

THE

JEWS

IN

Great Britain and *Ireland*,

On the same foot with all other Nations.

Containing also,

A Defence of the *Jews*

AGAINST

All vulgar Prejudices in all Countries.

Have we not all one Father? Has not one God created us? Why do we deal treacherously every one with his neighbour? Mal. 2. 10.

Utinam qui ubique sunt Propugnatores hujus Imperii, possent in hanc Civitatem venire, & contra Oppugnatores Reipublicae de Civitate exterminari. Cic. in Orat. pro L. Corn. Balbo. cap. 2.

LONDON:

Printed for *J. Roberts* in *Warwick-lane*. 1714.

Facsimile of the original edition, published as a pamphlet in December 1714. Source: Google Books

The Dedication

To the Most Reverend the

ARCH-BISHOPS,

And the Right Reverend the

BISHOPS,

of both Provinces.

May it please your graces and your lordships,

Two considerations have embolden'd me to make this address, your Piety and your Learning.

Your Piety not only leads you to promote the good of all mankind; even of your very enemies; but to look with particular eyes of affection upon the Jewish *Nation, to whom you are not ignorant what privileges and prerogatives peculiarly belong. By them you are undeniably come to the knowledge of one* GOD, *from them you have received the holy* Scriptures, *of them is descended* MOSES *and the* Prophets, *with* JESUS *and all the* Apostles*: nor is it from any other pattern or original, but their* Hierarchy, *that the distinguishing posts you now fill in the* Church, *can be illustrated or defended; and the same holds as true of* Liturgies, Tythes, Vestments, *and* Ceremonies.

YOUR Learning convinces You, that this people deserves not that Contemt under which they so *generally labor at present; since no other Nation can produce more authentic monuments of its rise and antiquity, of its religious and political State, nay, or of its military and heroic exploits. Tis true, that after undergoing various fortunes from the* Egyptians *and the* Persians, *they fell at last, with the better part of the World, under the irresistible force of the* Roman *Eagles. But their Conquerors soon became their * Captives. The* Jews *gave up their Arms to the Romans, and the Romans gave up their Understandings to the Jews; the nobler victory of the two. So did the learned* Egyptians, *so did the polite* Grecians, *so did the barbarous* Goths *and* Vandals*: the posterity of these, and of several other nations, being now more early made acquainted with the* Jewish *history, rites, and customs, than with those of their own Countries; and all of us proud to bear the proper Names of the very people, we no less inhumanly, than inconsistently hate and despise.*

BUT as by your Learning you further know how considerable a part of the British *inhabitants are the undoubted † off spring of the* Jews *(to which the old* Irish *can lay no claim) and how many worthy Prelates of this same flock, not to speak of Lords or Commoners, may at this time make an illustrious figure among us: so your Learning and Piety together, dispose you to procure the flourishing state of your Country, opposite to the pernicious maxims of those* Priests *your Predecessors; who, in the following piece, appear to have been the implacable enemies of the* Jews, *as their Superstition made them adversaries to true Religion. Nor did they ever appear for Liberty against an encroaching* Monarch *(as sometimes they have done) but because they wou'd not have the people fleec'd, by any Tyrants except themselves.*

CONSIDERING therefore your power in the Church, your authority in the Senate, and your influence upon all the People; to whom shou'd I preferably apply my self on the behalf of this Nation, whose abandoned cause I plead? For, whatever I may judge in my own mind of the success, I am not without hope I shall be judg'd by you, to have espous'd a righteous interest: as I am certain, your previous suffrage must engage in its favor the charitable part of the inferior Clergy, *and all the understanding men of the* Laity. *But after a review of those conspicuous virtues, which render you venerable even to the* Protestant Dissenters, *who cannot in conscience submit to your jurisdiction, I may not doubt,*

My Lords,

but that, as you are the advocates of the Jews at the Throne of Heaven, so you will be their friends and protectors in the British *Parliament.*

Farewell.

* O utinam nunquam Judaea subacta fuisset / Pompeii bellis, imperioque Titi! / Latius excisae gentis contagia serpunt, / Victoresque suos Natio victa premit. - Rutil.Itinerar. Lib. I.

† Vid. Pag. 37

Reasons for Naturalizing the Jews in Great Britain and Ireland.

As most Animals are immediately after their birth capable to provide for themselves, without any assistance from their own Species or others among their fellow-creatures; so we see that few of them preserve any ties of kindred, acquaintance, friendship, or confederacy together; there being no mutual obligations, dependance, or necessity long remaining, to produce or cement these duties. Such as are longer a bringing up by their dams, or forc'd to keep under the protection of their sires (as Horses for example) do the longer retain a visible kindness and distinction for them, and such as not only in their breeding want the help of their own Species, but all their lives after depend upon the good-will of some other (as we may remark in Dogs) do preserve a continual regard of love, obedience, friendship, and gratitude to that degree, as not seldom to expose their lives for their masters, or to pine sometimes even to death for the loss of their benefactors. But Man being longer a rearing than any other creature, and absolutely incapable to subsist afterwards without the company of other Men, contracts from the very beginning, not only the relations of father, mother, brothers, sisters, and other degrees of kindred, as those to whom he's first, and most, and longest indebted for his preservation or pleasure; but he likewise in process of time forms the notions of acquaintance, neighbourhood, friendship, affinity, association, confederacy, subjection, and superiority, as never being able, during his whole life, to subsist in any tolerable degree of security or delight, without the help of such. Tis therefore the duty of every Man to contribute as much as he can, whether by his advice or by his industry, to the welfare of his whole species, and particularly of his family; but in a special manner to the safe and flourishing condition of that country or society to which he immediately belongs, as in whose happiness his own is so necessarily involved.

II.

BEING always sensible of this obligation, I have in many instances done my uttermost to promote the good of my country, according as the circumstances or situation of my affairs wou'd permit me; and particularly, I have more than once or twice (as opportunity offer'd) enforc'd the usefulness and necessity of a GENERAL NATURALIZATION. This, after many oppositions from very different interests, was at last most happily brought to a conclusion: and, if I may not flatter myself to have had my share with others, in persuading and convincing some Persons to embrace the right side of the question; yet no body can deny me the satisfaction, of having judg'd aright in this momentous affair, and to have early asserted that, which the wisdom of a *Parliament* had afterwards pass'd into a publick Law. Nor am I the less in love with it for being since repeal'd by another *Parliament*; as many good Laws have often met with the like passionate and injurious treatment, that afterwards became essential parts of the Constitution. We must it's true, yield obedience to the Laws, however unwholesome, so long as they continue in force; but we are at full liberty to represent in a dutiful manner the inconvenience of any such Laws, as we may legally petition to have 'em repealed: and that so much the sooner, by how much better some rejected Laws may be esteem'd, particularly if the hasty repealing of them, proves to be a Satyr upon the very Understanding of the nation. This same Law however, in my humble opinion, was still incomplete, as most Laws are so at first; being afterwards occasionally, and by degrees, brought to their due perfection. I don't find fault with the late *Act of* GENERAL NATURALIZATION, because those were justly excluded from the benefits of it, who hold opinions diametrically inconsistent with our Government; such as the doctrine of dispensation from Oaths, the not tolerating of any *Churches* but their own, and the acknowledging a foreign Potentate, which they believe superior to our legal Soveraign: but I am sorry that the *Act* did not include all those who wou'd not only be good subjects, but who wou'd also be as useful and advantageous to the public Weal, as any of those *Protestant Churches*, to which it was then restrain'd. As soon as I declare I mean the *Jews*, it will be easily conceiv'd, that my principal aim is not be popular, however heartily I may serve my Country: and I am inexpressibly pleas'd, that the most effectual way to do so, is the promoting of Humanity, and the doing good to all Mankind.

III.

I KNOW it will be presently said, that I am a lover of Paradoxes; and others (if they please) may reckon for a Paradox any truth, which is ever so little remote from common observation, or that they have no mind shou'd be told. Nevertheless tis manifest almost at first sight, that the common reasons for a GENERAL NATURALIZATION, are as strong in behalf of the *Jews*, as of any other people whatsoever. They encrease the number of hands for labor and defence, of bellies and backs for consumption of food and raiment, and of brains for invention and contrivance, no less than any other nation. We all know that numbers of people are the true riches and power of any country, and we have been often told, that this is the reason, why *Spain* (since the expulsion of the *Jews* and *Moors*) being continually drain'd of her inhabitants by the colonies in *America*, and all other Nations being in a manner kept out by the rigor of the *Inquisition* is grown so prodigiously weak and poor: wheras, tho *Holland* has comparatively but few native Inhabitants, and lends great numbers yearly to the *East-Indies*, yet allowing an unlimited LIBERTY OF CONSCIENCE, and receiving all nations to the right of citizens, the country is ever well stockt with people, and consequently both rich and powerful to an eminent degree. Our own *Plantations*, and the excessive growth of the city of *London*, begun very sensibly to drain many of our counties, till, since the late happy Revolution, we made matters much easier to all men, both in respect of civil and religious privileges: and now that there is LIBERTY OF CONSCIENCE for most sorts of people (excepting such as are deservedly excluded from this blessing) I doubt not, but, upon making the NATURALIZATION more easy at least, the room of those will quickly be supply'd, who yearly go to the Plantations and in the service of the East-India Company; not to speak of our Armies, Fleets, or Adventurers. Nay more, I am fully persuaded that we shall get hands enow, not only for encreasing and improving all sorts of arts and manufactures; but for breaking up and cultivating those desert, yet not barren grounds, of which there is still but too great a quantity in *Scotland* and *Ireland* (and even in *England* it self) under the names of Heaths, Moors, Bogs, Fens, and Commons, to which may be likewise added, without offence, many of our Parks and Chases.

IV.

THE late colonies from the *Palatinate*, or rather that heterogeneous mixture of all sorts of Nations and Religions, who took their denomination from the greater number, is none of the examples I wou'd alledge to prove this assertion. The public-spirited part of that design was blasted and overborn by the artifice of such as hated the authors of it, being envious of any good these wou'd do their Country, and yet doing nothing for it themselves. Wou'd to God it cou'd be said, they had done nothing against it! Besides that the greatest share of those miserable wretches were allur'd hither on the foot of private interest, by *American* Proprietors or Planters; and not upon the prospect of any benefit they expected from the GENERAL NATURALIZATION, of which privilege the coming over of so many *Papists*, makes it plain they knew as little, as beggars of any persuasion cou'd be suppos'd to get by it. But I mean those other Strangers, very different in quality and circumstances, whether residing here before, or come over since the passing of the late *Act*, who have got themselves naturaliz'd, and are become no less useful by stocks and credit, than by their industry and callings. The tale of such is very considerable, and yet tis but a small beginning to larger numbers who are actually preparing to transport themselves into these fortunate Islands; tho not in such multitudes at a time as the *Palatines*, which made it inconvenient to the Government as well as to themselves. But there are people of quite another sort, who design to settle among; now that the legal entail of our Crown appears to be firmly fix'd to succeeding generations, in the numerous Lineage of our incomparable King GEORGE, I mean, in short, that there are several, who, having got considerable estates elsewhere, but invited by the Healthiness, Plenty, and Pleasantness of our Country (tho much more powerfully allur'd by envy'd freedom of our Government, the inviolable security of their goods and persons) do hope to lead here a more able and contented life, than they cou'd do at home; especially now, that, in case of a

NATURALIZATION, they may not only exercise Trade, and purchase Estates, without any national restrictions, but be admitted to Honours and Employments indiscriminably with natives. But I need not longer insist on this head, since the late repeated debates about the NATURALIZATION must needs have convinced those, who did not so well understand it before, and who might be too much transported by a national Paroxysm: for I am farr from imagining, that every one, who oppos'd it the first time, or that wou'd qualify, or were quite against it the last time, had an ill meaning to his country, or a private interest to biass him. The Seducers of some brethren are no less known, than the Accusers of others, they being the self-same trusty Gang. But I am truly concern'd, that there remains still among us so many notorious Prejudices against a GENERAL NATURALIZATION, and such as will amply serve to justify what I have hitherto discours'd in general on this subject, which wou'd otherwise seem to be superfluous. I shall now therefore come to a more particular application of these common Principles.

V.

MY Purpose at present then, is to prove, that the *Jews* are so farr from being an Excrescence or Spunge (as some wou'd have it) and a useless member in the Commonwealth, or being ill subjects, and a dangerous people on any account, that they are as obedient, peaceable, useful, and advantageous as any; and even more so than many others: which last point, as seeming the least probable, I shall briefly demonstrate in two or three respects. And, in the first place, it is evident, that by receiving of the *Jews*, no body needs be afraid that any religious Party in the nation will thereby be weaken'd or enforc'd. The *Protestant Dissenters* have no reason to be jealous, that they shou'd join with the *National Church* to oppress them, since they have an equal Interest to preserve LIBERTY OF CONSCIENCE; and that the example of *Spain* and *Portugal* has taught 'em how dangerous a thing it is, that one sett of *Clergy-men* shou'd dispose and influence all things at their pleasure in any country. The *National Church* on the other hand, has no reason to be jealous that the *Jews* shou'd come in for snacks with them in sharing the Ecclesiastical Benefices; so that no candidate or expectant from the *University* needs shew his zeal on this occasion, to keep the *Jews* out of the nation (as has been done once on a time to keep the *Dissenters* out of the *Church*) lest he shou'd be shoulder'd out of a Parish by some *Levite*, or be kept from a fat Bishoprick by a *Rabbi*. There's as little danger they shou'd ever join with any particular Body of *Dissenters* against the *National Church*, since they can expect no more favor from the one, than the other; and that it is always their interest to preserve the legal Establishment, on which their own Security is grounded. For this reason likewise, they'll never join with any Party in civil Affairs, but that which patronizes LIBERTY OF CONSCIENCE and the NATURALIZATION, which will ever be the side of

Liberty and the Constitution. But otherwise they are wholly devested of those engagements to WHIG and TORY, which are become hereditary in so many Families: and this holds as true of other Factions, which shou'd consequently recommend them to the favor of all Parties, wou'd people but think for themselves; and not, like so many Brutes, be led or driven by a few self- interested Demagogues.

VI.

ANOTHER Consideration that makes the *Jews* preferable to several sorts of People, is, their having no Country of their own, to which they might retire, after having got Estates here; or in favor of which, they might trade under the umbrage of our NATURALIZATION, which I am certain will be done by many, unless prevented by proper Laws: for I have known several get themselves naturalized before the late *Act*, yet without ever designing to live in *England*, or to become a part of the *English* Government; but to avoid in their Factorship paying Aliens duties, and for other reasons well known to the Merchants. But the *Jews* having no such Country, to which they are ty'd by inclination or interest as their own, will never likewise enter into any political engagements, which might be prejudicial to ours, as we have known (for Example) certain *French* Refugees to have done, notwithstanding their protection; nay, and to be ever pleas'd with any successes against us (which I say, without Prejudice to the more honest and more numerous part) as making for the greatness of their nation, wherein they full took a sort of pride, and to which, some of 'em are gone back again, after failing of their expectations here. The *Jews* therefore being better us'd with us, than any where else in the world, are sure to be ours for ever; which is more than we dare reasonably promise from any other nation, whatever may be expected from their posterity.

VII.

BUT to ascend from these particular to more general Reasons, we may observe that Trade is by certain circumstances shar'd in such a manner, and parcell'd out among the inhabitants of the earth, that some, by way of eminence, may be call'd the Factors, some the Carriers, some the Miners, others the Manufactorers, and others yet the Store-keepers of the world. Thus the *Jews* may properly be said to be the Brokers of it, who, whithersoever they come, create business as well as manage it. Yet it is neither by any National Institution or Inclination (as many ignorantly believe) that they do now almost entirely betake themselves to business of Exchange, Insurances, and improving of money upon Security; but they are driven to this way of Livelihood by mere Necessity: for being excluded every where in *Europe*, from publick Employments in the State, as they are from following Handycraft-trades in most places, and in almost all, from purchasing immovable Inheritances, this does no less naturally, than necessarily, force 'em to Trade and Usury, since otherwise they cou'd not possibly live. Yet let 'em once be put upon an equal foot with others, not only for buying and selling, for security and protection to their Goods and Persons; but likewise for Arts and Handycraft-trades, for purchasing and inheriting of estates in Lands and Houses (with which they may as well be trusted as with Shares in the *publick Funds*) and then I doubt not, but they'll insensibly betake themselves to Building, Farming, and all sorts of Improvement like other people. What I here assert, is by no means to be disprov'd from their present general occupation of *Exchange*, to which they are driven out of Necessity (as I have just now shewn) but not out of choice or inclination. They were originally Shepherds in *Mesopotamia*, Builders in *Egypt*, and Husbandmen in their own Country; all, or any of which, they may as well become in any other Land. They were strictly prohibited Usury among themselves by their Law, [Exod. 22. 25; Lev. 25. 36, 37; Deut. 23, 19, 20.] and but barely permitted to exercise it among Strangers: but however, it can no longer be made an objection by the *Christians*, since they practice it as generally themselves; and that the indigent Borrower will be sure to complain of the opulent Lender in all times and places, be the Premium he disburses ever so moderate. From undoubted Monuments we are assur'd, that the *Jews* were antiently excellent Soldiers. Their maritime Tribes produc'd as good Seamen. Both the one and the other follow'd these callings in the Service of foren Nations, particularly under the *Assyrian* and *Egyptian*, under the *Greec* and *Roman* powers. Now I ask any man, why they may not as well do the same (if lawfully made capable) in *Great Britain* and *Ireland*? And whether they may not navigate ships of their own, as in the time of SOLOMON; or serve in the ships of others, as they have done many times since ? There must indeed be an intermixture of other seamen, by reason of their *Sabbath*; tho the *Sabbath* perhaps by sea, was no more obligatory, than the *Sabbatical Year* by Land, out of *Judea*. But this is not a place to examine such points of antient Learning. I envy not those whole streets of magnificent buildings, that the *Jews* have erected at *Amsterdam* and the *Hague*: but there are other *Jews* enow in the World to adorn *London* or *Bristol* with the like, the fifth part of the People in *Poland* (to name no other Country,) being of this Nation. Nay, the very Original of their present numerous Settlement at *Prague* in *Bohemia* is a Privilege granted them in the tenth Century, to build a *Synagogue* there, as a recompence for the valiant assistance they lent the inhabitants, in expelling the invading and depopulating Barbarians: And I fancy they cou'd kill the enemies of our *British* Islands, when they become their own, with equal alacrity.

VIII.

I AM not ignorant how much the world is governed by prejudices, and how farr some, who wou'd not be counted of the vulgar, are yet sway'd by vulgar errors. One of the most general is the prevailing notion of a certain genius, or bent of mind, reigning in a certain Family or Nation. That there is in reality such a Biass frequently observable, I go not about to deny, but only maintain that it wholly proceeds from Accident, and not from Nature. The different methods of Government and Education, are the true springs and causes of such different inclinations all over the world, as it demonstrably appears from the progressive changes, which alterations in those two main points have effected in most countries, both of the modern and antient times. Compare the present *Greece* and *Italy* with the past; or even old *England* with the new, and you can doubt of the matter no longer. I reject not all that is attributed to the climate; but as Government and Education even get the better of that, so it is frequently chang'd by the inhabitants, and has been so for many ages by the *Jews*. If an *English* Cock or Mastiff transported hence, degenerates in the first **[illegible[1]]** there's no reason it shou'd not hold as true of the Men, at least in the second or third. As for the Jews in particular, whatever genius will be allowed to have influenc'd 'em in *Judea* (for I enter not here into that matter) tis evident, that since their dispersion, they have no common or peculiar inclination distinguishing 'em from others; but visibly partake of the Nature of those nations among which they live, and where they were bred. The ordinary sentiments and manners of the *Portuguese* or *Italian Jews*, differ not from those

1. From the context of this passage is would seem that the illegible word is 'case' - Editor's Note.

of the other *Portuguese* or *Italians*. The *Germans* differ from the *Popish*[2] *Jews*, as much as *Poles* do from *Germans*; and so do those of *Ispahan* or *Constantinople*, from such as are born at *London* or *Amsterdam*. Yet so strong is the force of prejudice, that I know a person, no fool in other instances, who labor'd to perswade me, contrary to the evidence of his own and my eyes (to mine I am sure) that every *Jew* in the world had one eye remarkably less than the other, which silly notion he took from the Mob. Others will gravely tell you, that they may be distinguish'd by a peculiar sort of smell, that they have a mark of blood upon one shoulder, and that they cannot spit to any distance, with a world of such extravagant fancies, exciting at once laughter, scorn, and pity.

IX.

THERE are among the *Jews*, to be sure, sordid wretches, sharpers, extortioners, villains of all sorts and degrees: and where is that happy nation, where is that religious profession, of which the same may not be as truely affirm'd? They have likewise their men of probity and worth, persons of courage and conduct, of liberal and generous spirits. But one rule of life, which is willingly admitted, nay, and eagerly pleaded by all Societies in their own case (tho

---

2. Sic. The term 'Popish' appears in the original edition but it seems certain that this is a misprint. Toland is obviously referring here to 'Polish Jews' - Editor's Note.

miserably neglected in that of others) is, *not to impute the faults of a few to the whole number*; which, considering the unavoidable mixture of good and bad in all communities, wou'd be no less want of charity, than want of justice. The *Jews* therefore are both in their origine and progress, not otherwise to be regarded, than under the common circumstances of human nature. The *Romans* were not less esteem'd for being descended from Shepherds and Fugitives (which original they had in common with the *Jews*) than are the *English* for being the progeny of barbarous pyrates, and a repeated mixture of several nations. Notwithstanding all this, so great is the aversion which diversity of manners in general begets among men, and especially contrary rites or doctrines of Religion, that, farr from mutual love and good offices, as creatures of the same species, they foolishly despise and hate one another for their civil customs, but cruelly persecute and murder one another on the score of their religious ones. All histories are full of such execrable examples. Defamation, Exile, Imprisonment, and Death, were sometimes not esteem'd punishments severe enough, for the neglect of ceremonies in their own nature indifferent, and very often insignificant; or from the disbelief of doctrines understood by neither party; and when understood, that contributed not a jot to make mankind the wiser or the better. On such accounts, the tombs of the dead have been often violated, their ashes thrown into the air, and their very names branded with infamy: the People being artfully wrought up to these excesses, when *Priests* or *Politicians* were to be gainers.

X.

BUT no people or sect in the world, has had sadder experience of these truths in all times, than the *Jews*: for their religious customs differing in the whole from all other nations, and being in the parts directly contrary to those of several, they had all nations therefore for their enemies; who agreed to plague and persecute them incessantly, however they might disagree in other things among themselves. What they suffer'd from the *Heathens*, may be learnt from the books of the *Old Testament*, from those we term with them *Apocryphal* from JOSEPHUS and PHILO, and not a few scantlings from the *Greec* and *Roman* Authors. But the *Annals* of all *European* nations are foully besmear'd with their blood, since *Christianity* got the mastery. It wou'd be endless to relate the havock that was made of their goods and persons in every country. Had the cruelties and barbarities exercis'd against them been only recorded by themselves, or by any other but *Christians*, that were coevous, eye-witnesses, and sometimes actors in those tragedies, I shou'd never have believ'd one half of 'em, nay, had one *Christian* Nation or Sect reported such things of their antagonist *Christians*, and that each Party had not agreed on the matter in their own books, not seldom glorying in the fact, I had been very cautious and backward in giving my assent. Very often they were massacred by thousands, without the least cause pretended. Any sense of humanity being cast off to such a degree, as if the *Jews* had been but silly sheep, and their enemies ravenous Wolves. At other times, ZEAL for the glory of God was alledg'd, which is the most terrible and bloody expression in any language, when a bigot speaks it. They were sometimes accus'd thro'out all *Europe*, of poysoning the waters in hatred to the *Christians*, for which, tho the thing be so improbable in wells, and in rivers impossible, twelve thousand suffer'd death in the city of *Mentz* alone. Intelligence with the *Saracens* and *Moors* was not seldom a plausible pretext. When a *Crusade* was proclaim'd against the *Turks*, contrary to the first principles of common Right, then with all the fury the Fryers cou'd inspire, those Soul-errant warriors, consecrated to blood and rapine, massacred the *Jews* without mercy, for a blessing on their undertaking at first setting out: and with all the cruelty of cowards they butcher'd 'em when they returned, especially if they got the worst on't, which they commonly did; as a dog will run at a stone, when he dares not attack the man that threw it. What need we go so farr abroad (said they) to fight the *Mahometan* enemies of the cross, when we may on much cheaper Terms merit heaven, by destroying the cursed *Jews* at home? Thus were they treated every where, Princes seldom granting 'em liberty, but in order to rob 'em when they grew rich: and this they did with the greater security, because nobody assisted or pity'd them, and that all others were glad to be eas'd at their expence. *The Zeal of the* Christians (says

HENRY * DE KNYGHTON,) *conspir'd against the* Jews, *but in truth not sincerely, that is, for the cause of Faith; but either out of emulation or envy, because of their felicity, or out of gapeing after their goods, the justice of God not at all approving such things.*

* De Eventibus Angliae, l.2 c. 13.

XI.

BUT their most inveterate Enemies were the *Priests*, who devoutly offer'd up those human Sacrifices, not only to share their Goods with the rapacious *Prince*, but also to acquire the reputation of zeal and sanctity among the credulous vulgar. Every thing, in short, tho ever so false or impossible, serv'd for a handle good enough to rifle, or expel, or slaughter the *Jews*. The very suffering of them to live, was by the Preachers of those Times, made to be the cause of plagues, and famine, and every other disaster, that happened in the course of nature; and this too, where no *Jews* had ever been settl'd. They generally past for sorcerers: and the *Hebrew* Letters, which the ignorant Monks cou'd not read, were given out by them to be magic characters. One pretence was as generally us'd against them, as now you find throwing of stones related in stories of haunted houses, or vomiting of pins in witchcraft; and this (forsooth) was the stealing of a Child to crucify him against *Easter*, and to eat his heart by way of opproby to JESUS. This has been alleg'd against them a thousand times, and many thousands have suffer'd for it. Yet not only BERNARD, Abbot of *Clairval* (afterwards sainted) undertook their defence, but even several *Popes* acknowledg'd such accusations to be invidious calumnies, and seriously deplor'd their misery. GREGORY the ninth's two Letters on this subject may be read in RAYNALDUS: as also that of INNOCENT the fourth (to name no more) which acquits them of this particular Cruelty towards innocent children, showing that their Law, [Gen. 9. 4; Lev. 17 10, 15; Deut 12. 16, 23 & 15. 23] their most tremendous Law against the eating of any Blood, is contrary to such a Practice; and their condition under Princes was farr worse than that of their forefathers under PHARAO. I wonder not so much, that diverse *Emperors* out of their Lay-pity shou'd ofte endeavour to protect them, which, notwithstanding all their might, and even in conjunction with the *Popes*, they were not always able to do: so dangerous and destructive a monster is SUPERSTITION, when rid by the *Mob*, and driven by the *Priests*, not seldom to the overthrow of those, who let it loose on quite other designs. Our second JOSEPHUS, the reverend Mons. BANAGE, with some other learned and moderate *Protestant* Divines, have likewise undeniably prov'd this murder of Children to be a gross fable, invented out of perfect malice and calumny. The *Christians* themselves at their first setting out in the world were not more candidly treated by the *Heathens*, who charg'd them with this very crime of Child-eating; which has been so farr from making them charitable to others or one another, that, not to insist on the execrable practices attributed to such as they call the *primitive Heretics*, they do now at the springing up of any new Sects, make use of the very same artifice, accusing 'em of I know not what disorders. But to stick to the *Jews*, dead Bodies were frequently thrown into their houses, when they least knew of it. If a wafer or a crucifix tainted with blood, were purposely laid (as was often done) in the corner of a Church, or in any other place where they were sure to be found, a fanatical *Fryer* needed but shew it with ridiculous gesticulations to the people, who presently ran, without any other proof or declaration, to plunder and massacre the *Jews*, to burn their houses and their *synagogues*: nor did such pious practices fail of being approved by other miracles, believ'd to be no less authentic than the former. This is the never-failing effect of letting the *Clergy* meddle in state-affairs. Now leaving the Reader to collect what he pleases of this sort in the histories of other nations, I'll present him with the following instances, out of many others in our *Annals*, concerning the hard usage of this miserable people, whom I wou'd have as easily naturalized as any others: for I am not asham'd to say with PLINY, that * *I desire the greatness of my Country in all respects, but more especially in the increase of Citizens, which make the true strength and ornament of towns* in a free country.

* Cupio enim Patriam noftram omnibus quidem rebus augeri, maximè tamen Civium numero id enim oppidis firmissimum ornamentum. Lib. 7. Ep. 32.

XII.

FROM the time that WILLIAM the Conqueror first brought the *Jews* from *Roan* in *Normandy* into this Kingdom, in the Year 1070, they suffer'd in their goods and persons all the horrible things that Priests and Politicians cou'd devise; some of both orders having too scrupulous a conscience, and others none at all. King WILLIAM was too wise a prince, knew too well of what importance they were to his new-acquir'd Dominion, to use 'em ill; and our succeeding Kings (who had a sort of property in them) drew a very considerable Revenue from these *Jews*, by more Ways than one, and by some that were unjust enough: so that tis amazing how numerous they grew in spite of all partiality and severities; not a town of any note in the whole Kingdom (one or two excepted) that had not in it a *Synagogue*, or a good many *Jewish* inhabitants. We read of several of both sexes among 'em, that were exceeding rich in land as well as in mony, in fees, in mortgages, and in purchases. There was even a particular *Exchequer of the Jews*, where all receipts and issues, arising on their account, were manag'd: and the Judges of this Exchequer, or as then stil'd, the *Justices of the Jews*, consisted partly of *Jews* and partly of *Christians*, who are often mention'd by their proper names and titles in our history. But their condition, for all this, was little to be envy'd; since upon default of any payment, justly or unjustly impos'd, they us'd frequently to be all arrested at once, with their wives, and children, and servants: and they were not seldom forc'd to forgive the debts that were owing to them by others. Whoever is desirous to be more particularly inform'd about this matter, may abundantly satisfy his curiosity in the no less accurate and laborious, than useful and entertaining *History of the Exchequer*, by MR. MADOX. But the instances I am going to produce are most of 'em on a religious account, and such especially are gathered out of other Historians, who relate the causes or pretences of these persecutions. WILLIAM RUFUS, who was no bigot in Religion, favor'd them for the same political reasons that his father brought them over; and became mortally hated by the *Clergy*, not only for want of a blind veneration towards themselves, but also for always granting a fair hearing to the *Jews*, even in religious disputations with the *Priests*. HENRY the first continu'd their protector on the same good grounds with his father and brother; and in the contests between MAUD and STEPHEN, neither side had leisure to mind them much, either for good or evil. HENRY the second, in the thirty third Year of his Reign, seiz'd upon the fourth part of their Chattels by way of Tallage, says MR. MADOX; and not seldom they had but one part in three left 'em. Yet this King, with whom ended WILLIAM the first's political Scheme, was no enemy to the *Jews*.

XIII.

BUT in RICHARD the first's time, they were not only robb'd of all they had in *Norwich*, *Lyn*, *Stamford*, and other cities, where many of them were piteously murder'd, chiefly at the instigation of the *Clergy*; but also in *London* and *Westminster*, where they were most barbarously us'd on the very Coronation-day, some of 'em being knock'd o' the head in the very Church, under pretence of bewitching the King. As if all their nation had been accomplices in this pretended enchantment, the word was given out, and the Zealots (which were observ'd to be the leudest ignorantest fellows of the Kingdom) straight fell upon them without any mercy. At *York* five hundred of them were besieg'd in a tower of the Royal Castle, and the ransom they offer'd for their lives being refus'd, they did (out of despair, and to avoid greater cruelty from their enemies) first kill their wives and children, and then burnt the house wherein they were, together with themselves: an act that wou'd be counted heroic in *Romans*, *Greecs*, or *Carthaginians*; nor is the like disapprov'd in SAMSON, or the * adherents of the MACCABEES. After this Massacre the *Christian* inhabitants very honestly discharg'd their own debts, by the pillage and obligations of the *Jews*. King JOHN, who was so noisom and mischievous to his own subjects, cou'd not fail of putting those wretches to all manner of torments and vexations, that they might be oblig'd to ransom themselves, as then was the language and practice. Every one of them (says STOW) had one Eye pull'd out at least; and one in particular had a tooth pull'd out every day for seven days together, till he ransom'd the residue with ten thousand marks of silver, all the *Jews* paying at that time sixty thousand marks. But when this King and his *Barons* broke out into civil wars, their case was most deplorable between both; for when the *Barons* enter'd *London* by force, they search'd the coffers of the *Jews* (says the same STOW) to stuff their own purses that had been long empty, and to engratiate their faction with the *Clergy*. In King HENRY the third's time, after they had been permitted to build a sumtuous *Synagogue* at their own expence, it was, at the request of idle and useless *Monks*, unjustly taken from them, consecrated to the Virgin MARY, and is now St. ANTHOLIN'S Church, rebuilt since the dreadful fire. In the same reign, under the thread bare pretence of stealing a child at *Norwich* to crucify him, their bodies and goods were adjudg'd to be at the King's disposal, who made the best of this bargain for himself, yet to be endur'd, had he not shed innocent blood. At another time he took from one AARON, a *Jew* born at *York*, fourteen thousand marks for himself, and ten thousand for the Queen; afterwards thirty thousand marks of silver for himself, and two hundred marks of gold for the Queen. Another of 'em, call'd ABRAHAM, redeemed himself for 7000 marks. In the same reign likewise one hundred and two *Jews*, still under the stale pretence of crucifying a child, were brought prisoners from *Lincoln* to *London*, where eighteen of 'em were hang'd. Four times in five Years were they accus'd of this crime, without the least foundation.

* ELEAZAR and RAZIS, I Mac. 6. 43-46, 2 Mac, 14.37-46.

XIV.

KING HENRY and his *Clergy* were not their only enemies; for, as it happen'd in King JOHN'S time, the *Barons*, that were in Arms against HENRY, slew the *Jews* in all places without mercy. There were murder'd at *London* to the number of seven hundred: the rest were stript of all they had, and their *Synagogue* defac'd, because a *Jew* wou'd force a *Christian* to pay more than two pence for the use of twenty shillings a week. King EDWARD the first, after forbidding 'em Usury, which was bidding 'em starve, executed two hundred and sixty seven of 'em at onetime for Clipping, of which crime it is improbable they shou'd be all guilty; and caus'd several of 'em at *London* to be drawn at horse-tails and hang'd, for the pretended crucifying of a child by others of their Nation at *Northampton*. They were moreover accus'd of a design to fire this last Town, together with the City of *London*, which was the most unlikely story that cou'd be invented; since these were the two places that harbor'd most of their nation, and where they were observ'd to thrive best. Next, the King order'd their *Synagogues* (which then were many) to be pull'd down, and being in want of mony in *France*, he caus'd all the *Jews* in England to be apprehended in one day, and to redeem themselves for twelve thousand pounds of silver. At last, after inhumanities not to be mention'd without horror, he banish'd 'em quite of the Kingdom in the Year 1290; and the number of those that went away amounting to sixteen thousand, five hundred, and eleven, their houses and possessions were all sold, and brought a great sum of mony into the Exchequer, besides the grants made out of them by the King to his favorites and the *Clergy*. It ought not to be forgot, that the master of a Ship expos'd all of 'em that he had aboard, on the sands in the *Thames* mouth, where they miserably perish'd. The Pretences for this usage from the King were several, all promoted by a *Synod* held at *London*; but among others it was alledg'd, that a *Priest*, to obtain the love of a fair *Jewess*, had renounced both his orders and his religion, became circumcised, and actually marry'd to her: for no revolution happens in the world without a *Woman* or a *Priest* at the bottom of it, and here you have both in the Intrigue.

XV.

THUS were the Jews expell'd at once, after they had continu'd here 220 Years: and never surffer'd to return again, till in the time of the late civil wars they were admitted by OLIVER CROMWELL, who had the spirit, tho not the right of Government. In King CHARLES the second's reign, they were conniv'd at and tolerated, but not authoriz'd by Charter or Act of Parliament: nor are they on any other terms than permission to this day, tho they have deserv'd much better by their obedience and affection to the Government, towards the support of which, their purses have been always open. This Banishment of the *Jews* made as great a noise then in the world, as did the like Banishment of 'em long after out of *Spain*; and they were both equally against the common good, as they were both procur'd by the incessant bawling of the *Priests* in each Nation. Some few of the *English Jews* had from time to time chang'd their religion before, what is now the *Rolls* in *Chancery-lane*; having been the seminary of such Conversions, or the *Convert-house*, which was endow'd for their maintenance: but many of 'em on this sad occasion chose rather to turn *Christians*, than to leave their sweet native Country to starve in a foren land; besides that the King took away from them and detain'd all their children under six years of age, which must have given rise to abundance of Families. Yet now, the posterity of these derive their pedigrees from the *Saxons* (forsooth) from the *Danes*, or from the *Normans*, except two or three families at most, who, I am told, are not asham'd to own they are descended from the farr antienter Nation. A great number of 'em fled to *Scotland*, which is the reason so many in that part of the Island, have such a remarkable Aversion to pork and black-puddings to this day, not to insist on some other resemblances easily observable. But the *Jews* again, on their readmittance into *Great Britain*, made extraordinary rejoicings every where, observing it as a sort of new Æra, keeping ever since an annual feast in commemoration of such a blessing; and I have a very handsom Poem that was penn'd on this subject by * *Barrios*.

* Epistle to Kahal Kados (that is, the Holy Church) at London.

XVI.

NOW, what ought to rejoice us all, those of our own Nation are not only long since devested of such barbarous and bloody practises, but likewise have by very sensible degrees (tho not so farr as might be wish'd) quitted certain narrow and bigotted principles, not more contrary to common humanity and genuine religion, than to their own public and private interest. Our political Contentions, both the sign and support of Liberty, are no contradiction to this assertion. The vulgar, I confess, are seldom pleased in any country with the coming in of Foreners among 'em: which proceeds, first, from their ignorance, that at the beginning they were such themselves; secondly, from their grudging at more persons sharing the same trades or business with them, which they call *taking the bread out of their mouths*; and, thirdly, from their being deluded to this aversion by the artifice of those who design any change in the Government. But as wise Magistrates will prevent the last, and are sensible of the first, so they know the second cause of the people's hatred, to be the true cause of the land's felicity; and therfore, not minding those, who mind nothing but their selfish projects, they'll ever highly encourage a confluence of strangers. We deny not that there will thus be more tailors and shoomakers; but there will be also more suits and shoes made than before. If there be more weavers, watchmakers, and other artificers, we can for this reason export more cloth, watches, and more of all other commodities than formerly: and not only have 'em better made by the emulation of so many workmen, of such different Nations, but likewise have 'em quicker sold off, for being cheaper wrought than those of others, who come to the same market. This one Rule of MORE, and BETTER, and CHEAPER, will ever carry the market against all expedients and devices. But to these reasons we may further add, that the same vulgar, who are so averse to the coming in of poor strangers, are as well pleas'd with the rich, which will generally hold true of the *Jews*; who moreover do always take care of their own poor, wherever they are, and cannot therfore be said (according to our country phrase just now cited) *to eat the bread out of the mouths of others*. All these advantages are yet more evident with respect to the product of Lands, which *shews* (to use the * words of Mr. LOCKE) *how much* NUMBERS OF MEN *are to be preferr'd to* LARGENESS OF DOMINIONS*; and that the* INCREASE OF LANDS, *and the right employment of them, is the great* END OF GOVERNMENT. *That Prince (says he) who shall be so wise and god-like, as by* ESTABLISH'D LAWS OF LIBERTY, *to secure protection and encouragement to the* HONEST INDUSTRY *of* *mankind, against the* Oppression of Power, *and the* Narrowness of Party, *will quickly be too hard for his Neighbours.* Such a Prince thou hast upon the throne, O *Britain'* as a General Naturalization is your peculiar interest, ye men of fruitful acres.

* A manuscript addition He left in the margin to Paragraph 43, of his incomparable Essay concerning the true Original, Extent, and End of Civil Government.

XVII.

THAT the encrease of people encreases import and export, garrisons and armies, with the tillage that feeds, and the revenues that pay 'em, is, I hope, no longer a doubt or secret to any. But tis only in order the more speedily and effectually to bring these things to pass, that I plead at present for the Naturalization Of The Jews. This once accomplish'd, I have reason not only to believe that they'll fall to building, husbandry, navigation, and purchasing (as I hinted before) but that they'll come in greater numbers than other people from all countrys hither. In several places they are still very hardly treated, tho their throats are not so familiarly cut as formerly. They are generally expos'd to the affronts and rapine of the Soldiery with impunity; wheras they wou'd be safe from all such rude Insults in the peaceable arms of *Britannia*. I have been in several Cities, where they are infamously lock'd up every night, in a quarter by themselves, under a peculiar guard, as at *Prague*; and in others, as at *Colen*, they are not permitted to dwell within the City, but whenever they come over from *Deuts*, on t'other side the *Rhine*, they must pay so much for every hour they continue in the town, which they must also leave before Sunset, wheras, if the Citizens of *Colen* understood their own interest, they shou'd rather give 'em immunities and privileges, with a *Synagogue* into the bargain, in order to inhabit among 'em. What a paltry fisher-town was *Leghorn*, before the admission of the *Jews*? What a loser is *Lisbon*, since they have been lost to it? I name these cities only for example-sake, having been a witness to such preposterous politics in many others. They are in most places forc'd to wear a distinct habit, as they do yellow hats at *Rome*, and red ones at *Venice*; they are often taxt for their passage, and lie under a great many other partial regulations. Tis true, that in *Turky* they enjoy immoveable property, and exercise mechanic arts; they have likewise numerous Academies in *Poland*, where they study in the *Civil* and *Canon Laws* of their nation, being privileged to determine even certain criminal Causes among themselves: yet they are treated little better than Dogs in the first place, and are often expos'd in the last to unspeakable Calamities.

XVIII.

NOW the worse they are us'd on the foresaid and the like accounts in any country, the more they'll be dispos'd to transport themselves hither, where already they live promiscuously with the other Citizens, and without any distinction of habit, or imposition of tribute. They have neither many lucrative employments, nor immoveable possessions to quit in other places, excepting the latter in *Holland*; wheras here they may hope for both, and being once with us, will never leave us: since they cannot be allur'd by ampler privileges from any nation besides; or at least if they be, it must needs be solely our fault. Let no man mistake what I have said of employments: for in the *Church*, as I have shown above, they'll accept of none; and they are as much excluded from most preferments in the *State*, by reason of certain forms of oaths, and some other conditions, which consistently with their religion they cannot perform. But there are offices, where such qualifications are not requir'd; and which may indifferently be held by men of all religions, as many in the *Exchequer*, *Customs*, and *Excise*, nor can I see any reason, why the *Jews* may not be employ'd in several Affairs in the city, as to be Directors of the *Bank*, of the *East India Company*, or the like; and we know the nature of mankind to be such, as not seldom to be ambitious of even expensive employments, for the credit of the honor or the trust. In how many places, since their dispersion (tho not so frequently of late) have they enjoy'd considerable posts and offices? They have in some been *first Ministers*, *high Treasurers* in many, and *Envoys* in most. The Emperor CONSTANTINE did by public Edict permit the *Jews* to exercise magistracy, as to be *Decurions* or Aldermen at *Triers* and *Colen*:

which same privilege was granted 'em before, to be enjoy'd all over the world, by the Emperor ALEXANDER SEVERUS. In a word, they ought to be so naturalized in *Great Britain* and *Ireland*, as, like the *Quakers*, to be incapacitated in nothing, but where they incapacitate themselves. A GENERAL NATURALIZATION, and a TOTAL INCAPACITY from Offices, are perfect inconsistencies: for as one, who understood this matter very well, * says, *If few have been found ever since mankind existed, that wou'd for their own native country, without the expectation of any reward, expose their bodies to the weapons of their enemies; do you think there may be such a person found that will undergo dangers for another Government, where not only he receives no reward, but that he is absolutely excluded from any?* But the privilege of purchasing alone (especially since Titles are like to be generally secur'd by the gradual Introduction of *Registers*) will be the most powerful motive to bring the richest of the *Jews* hither: for it may be easily demonstrated, that the want of immoveable property is the true Reason, and not any pretended Curse or other ridiculous fancy, why none of the vast Estates they so frequently acquire, seldom or ever descends to the third Generation; but arc always floating and unfixt, which hinders their families from growing considerable, and consequently deprives them of the credit and authority, wherof all men of worth may be laudably ambitious.

* Etenim cum pro sua Patria pauci post genus hominum natum repertisint, qui, nullis praemus propofitis, vitam suam hostium telis objecerint, pro aliena Republica quemquam fore putatis qui se opponat periculis, non modo nullo proposito praemio, sed etlam interdicto. *Cic. Orat. pro L. Corn. Balbo, cap. 10.*

XIX.

LET us therfore take advantage herein, as we have prudently done in other things, from the false measures of some other nations, and not suffer our selves to be gull'd by any specious pretences of policy or piety: as I cou'd tell of a certain City, where, when the *Jews*, from their good opinion of the situation, intended to settle themselves, the ringleading *Minister* made such passionate Declamations against the receiving those enemies of the Cross, as mov'd the peoples Zeal (that is to say, their fury) to a degree the Magistrates durst not controll: the sign of a very weak administration. The *Jews* hereupon retiring thence, were invited on very honorable conditions, and with offers of large privileges, to a neighboring City, which ows no small part of its present grandeur to those people. The infamous preacher of the first City dying some years after, it was by certain papers plainly discover'd, that not the spirit of God, but a pension from the last City, which was the real occasion of all those thundring *Sermons*, or spiritual harangues wherby, the *Jews* were driven away, to return. His country has his memory to this hour in abhorrence, but tis too late to repent: and therfore let countries take heed in time, how they suffer such *Incendiaries*, either in this or any other instance, to get a head, they may be sure that *Hirelings* wou'd not run any hazard, or be at so great pains for nought; as they may with no less certainly discover who pays 'em, by considering who gets or loses by their success in deluding the people.

XX.

I COU'D insist on several other as cogent Topics, as any that have been hitherto alledg'd, in behalf of the *Jews* but lest what I have already asserted about the benefit and safety of naturalizing them, shou'd be thought to proceed (tho on an honest principle) from my ignorance of their rites or genius, about which however I have taken no inconsiderable pains; and also to supply those other arguments by me purposely omitted, I shall in a convenient time publish the translation of a Treatise out of *Italian*, written above 60 years ago, by the famous Rabbi, SIMON LUZZATTO. This piece was offer'd with an intention near akin to mine, to the most serene Republic of *Venice*, where some hardships were then propos'd to be put upon the *Jews*, but by this means diverted. LUZZATTO was a man of extraordinary learning and judgment, very acute, and not meanly eloquent; which shows that the *Jews* want not always for able men, tho he gives excellent reasons himself, why the number of such is not great among them now, which wou'd equally happen to any other people under the same circumstances. I shall not anticipate what he so prudently discourses concerning inhabitants, trade, circulation of mony, rotation of offices, or the like; neither will I enter upon the particular apologies, which, with no less probability than capacity, he makes for his nation against divers sorts of imputations and prejudices. In general he defends them against the calumnies of the celebrated Historian, CORNELIUS TACITUS, and in particular, against three sorts of enemies, which they never fail'd to have in all countries. These are first the *zealots*, under whom may be listed *Priests* and *Hypocrites*; secondly *Politicians*, comprehending *corrupt States-men*, and *drivers of private Interest*; and thirdly the *vulgar*, who, under colour of *religion* or the *public good*, are acted, animated, and deluded by the other two, the better to serve their own sinister purposes.

XXI.

BUT, what more deserves our consideration, LUZZATTO shows, that the *Jews* are not only at this time not desirous, but that they were at no time oblig'd to propagate their Religion by force of arms; nor were ever discharg'd from the ties of humanity and reciprocal friendship, towards other nations on a religious account. Nay, if his assertions hold good (as I doubt not but they will) they wholly lose their pains, who so pompously labor to show that the *Jewish* religion was not made for all times and places, which, it seems, the professors of it never affirm; so that such disputants fight with their own shadows, or set up an adversary of their own arming, the easier to subdue him. LUZZATTO expresly maintains, that as their religion, consider'd as it is *Jewish*, or distinct from the LAW OF NATURE, was solely calculated for their own Nation and Republic; so they were never commanded to instruct others in their peculiar rites and ceremonies, tho they are every where enjoin'd to magnify to all the world the divine goodness, wisdom, and power, with those duties of men, and other attributes of God, which constitute NATURAL RELIGION. Among innumerable passages of the *old Testament*, that favor this doctrine, he cites the eleventh verse of the first chapter of MALACHY, where this Prophet, in the person of JEHOVAH, says, *From the rising of the Sun, even unto the going down of the same, my name is great among the nations; and in every place incense is offered unto my name, and a pure offering: for my name is great among the nations, says the Lord of Hosts.* The substantive verb not being here exprest (according to an ordinary usage of the *Hebrew* Language,) the *Jews* supply it in the present tense, and the *Christians* in the future: so that where the one reads *my name is great among the nations,* or *incense is offer'd unto my name*; the other reads, *my name* shall be *great among the nations*, and *incense* shall be *offer'd unto my name*; where I must do justice to the honesty of our *English* Translators, who in this passage, as well as in some others of the like nature, have caus'd the verb *shall be* to be printed in a different Letter, as not being to be found in the original. For my part, it is not my business to show, which of 'em follows the true construction, or which of 'em serves their adopted hypothesis; but only to express the current opinion of the *Jews*, in relation to the religious state of the *Gentiles*, which they inferr from this, and several other places of the *Old Testament*, with infinitely more charity than the bulk of *Christians*, who damn without exception all that receive not the *Old Testament* or the *New*, and, since the publishing of the last, involving the followers of the first in the same cruel sentence. Such *Christians* as assert the possibility of the *Heathen's* salvation, allow the privilege but to a few extraordinary persons; and commonly accompany their notion with all the cautions of a Paradox, which very modesty betokens the meanness of their number.

XXII.

TIS certain, on the other hand, that the *Jews* never excluded the vertuous *Gentiles* from heaven, no more than one sett of *Gentiles* did all or any other people in the world. Some *Christians* only of all mankind, have establish'd the DAMNING THEOLOGY, as if the usefulness or necessity of their Religion cou'd not be inferr'd without it: nor are these more charitable to one another, part of 'em expresly damning all other *Christians*, but those of their own Communion; and such Communions, as will not use this harsh language, yet declaring that the state of all others is at least very perillous, if not restraining Salvation in effect, tho not in words, to the few elect of their cant and livery. But LUZZATTO (that we may not forget him) does with all his brethren conclude, as well from the nature of the thing, as from passages like to that above cited, that tho the *Jews* had the best form of Religion deliver'd to them, and to which were to proselyte, not force, their servants in *Judea*, and the strangers that shou 'd inhabit among 'em there; yet the rest of the world was not left *Revelation*, *Miracles*, and *Prophets*, as may be seen by the instances of MELCHISEDECK, BALAAM, JETHRO and JOB: wou'd NAOMI (according to them) ever persuade her daughter in law RUTH, [Ruth 1.15] to go back again to her own People and Gods, had she been persuaded there was no salvation out of the Pale of the *Jewish* Church. To say no more on this subject, the *Jews* do maintain in their books, what I had confirm'd to me out of the mouths of many learned Rabbins, that were they now in full possession of their old Government and Country, they wou'd not endeavor to convert all the world to their THEOCRACY; the rest of the nations not being concern'd in their commemorative rites, peculiarly relating to the History of the *Israelites*. Thus the feast of the *Passover* signifies their escape out of *Egypt*, and theirs only; the feast of *Tabernacles*, their living under tents in the wilderness, and so of the rest. Very few, even of their nearest Neighbours, cou'd conveniently come three times a year to *Jerusalem*, with the like injunctions, impossible to be observ'd by others; which makes 'em admire their Religion shou'd be thought to concern all the world. And therefore they wou'd expect no more from the rest of mankind living out of *Judea* than, avoiding and detesting the worship of dead men, with all other sorts of Idolatry, to acknowledge and honor one supreme Being, or FIRST CAUSE, and to obey the LAW OF NATURE, as the adequate rule of their lives and manners. Did all the world profess this doctrine uncorrupted, and conscientiously observe this practice (tho attended with any rites not cruel, impure, or prophane) the *Jews* wou'd not onely hold the possibility of their salvation, but look upon them likewise as brethren, notwithstanding these shou'd not reciprocally own their particular REVELATION; yet abstaining always from offering any affront to their worship, which indeed no body ought to do to any people, nor in any case: and the Jews are peremtorily commanded by their Legislator, *not to revile the Gods of other nations.* [Exod. 22. 28.]

XXIII.

I ONLY briefly touch on such points of controversy, not as being (on this present occasion) concern'd in the issue, but as they directly conduce to the NATURALIZATION I propose; this doctrine rendring the *Jews* much more safe and sociable than is commonly imagin'd, all fear of making Proselytes being thus quite remov'd. And were it not for this necessary explication, I make no question, but, on the publishing of this Apology, we shou'd be told strange stories of *the danger of Judaizing*, by those, who in their Souls believ'd not a word of the matter.

The Author, at least, wou'd be represented as more than liable to suspicion; and tis well, if he were not oblig'd to submit to *a writ of Inspection*. But we know the men and their way, and therfore but little value their censure. So leaving 'em for this time to give an account of my actions to the public, I own, that thus much I thought necessary to write, for the common benefit on this uncommon subject; and if I shou'd not meet with a general applause (in which case I shall not at all be disappointed) yet I cannot but enjoy the particular satisfaction of having discharged what I believ'd to be my duty: since with all wise and honest men, Humanity and good Nature are sure to atone for any defect in my Politics. For the rest, since LUZZATTO'S book is full of *Quotations* out of antient authors, I shall insert the original of such passages in the margin; as also some necessary *Annotations*, historical and theological, but especially political, considering the difference between the *Venetian Republic* (for which the book was calculated) and our *British Government*, which since that time is much alter'd for the better. I must advertise the philological reader that he's to receive no less satisfaction from this book, than the political. The Chapter (for example) which treats of *the present state of Learning among the* Jews, is much the handsomest and most reasonable discourse, that ever I read on the subject. Nor can you any where besides, find a juster or more distinct account of those three principal ranks of Doctors, which subsist now among 'em: that is to say, first, the *Rabbins*, or *Talmudists*, and *Traditionaries*; secondly, the *philosophical Divines*, *Expounders*, or *Moralists*; and thirdly, the *Cabalists*, or *Professors of secrets*, and *Explainers of Mysteries*.

FINIS.

Further Reading

Justin Champion: 'Toleration and Citizenship in Enlightenment England: John Toland and the Naturalization of the Jews, 1714-1753' in *Toleration in Enlightenment Europe* by Ole Peter Grell, Roy Porter (editors), Cambridge University Press, 1999. ISBN: 978-0521651967

JN Duggan: *John Toland: Ireland's Forgotten Philosopher, Scholar ... and Heretic*, 2010. ISBN: 978-1-907522-08-6.

Jonathan Karp: *The Mosaic Republic in Augustan Politics: John Toland's 'Reasons for Naturalizing the Jews'*. Available to read and download online from the website of Hebraic Political Studies. http://www.hpstudies.org/20/article.aspx?articleid=37

Chronology: John Toland, his life and times

1066 William the Conqueror leads Norman conquest of England. Jews from Rouen arrive in England. No evidence of Jewish people residing in England prior to this date.

1079 The Annals of Inisfallen record "Five Jews [thought to be merchants from Normandy] came from over sea with gifts to Toirdelbach [king of Munster], and they were sent back again over sea."

1232 First indications of a Jewish community in Ireland. A grant by King Henry III to Peter de Rivel gives him the office of Treasurer and Chancellor of the Irish Exchequer, the king's ports and coast, and also "the custody of the King's Judaism in Ireland."

1290 King Edward I issues edict expelling all Jews from England

1496 Following expulsion from Portugal, groups of Marrano Jews settle on Ireland's south coast. One of them, William Annyas, was elected as mayor of Youghal, County Cork, in 1555. There was also Francis Annyas (Ãnes) a three time Mayor of Youghal in 1569, 1576 and 1581.

1638 *Discorso circa il stato de gl' hebrei et in particolar dimoranti nell'inclita città di Venetia* (Discourse on the Condition of the Jews) by Simone Luzzatto published.

1656 James Harrington proposes Jewish readmission to Britain as a whole, including the colonisation of Ireland with Jews.

1657 Oliver Cromwell encourages Jews to return to England

1659 *The Art of Lawgiving* by James Harrington.

1660 Ireland's first synagogue founded near Dublin Castle.

1670 John Toland born November 30th.

1677 William of Orange marries Mary Stuart.

1685 Charles II dies, succeeded by James II.
Revocation of the Edict of Nantes.

1686 John Toland joins Church of Ireland.

1687 Toland goes to Glasgow University.

1688 William of Orange invades England.

1689 William and Mary crowned King and Queen of England. Beginning of Nine Years War.

1690 Williamite War in Ireland. The Battle of the Boyne marks the turning point though the war itself was not concluded until 1691.

1696 *Christianity not Mysterious* published.

1697 *An Apology for Mr. Toland* published, also *A Defence of Mr Toland in a letter to Himself.*

1698 Toland's *The Life of John Milton* published.

1699 *Amyntor; or a defence of John Milton* published.

1700 *The Oceana and Other Works of James Harrington, with an Account of His Life by John Toland* published.

1701 Act of Settlement is passed. Toland accompanies Lord Macclesfield to Hanover.
Anglia Libera: or The Limitation and Succession of the Crown of England explained and asserted by John Toland is published.

1702 William of Orange dies, succeeded by Queen Anne.
War of the Spanish Succession begins.
Toland in Berlin.

1704 Toland's *Letters to Serena* published.
Battle of Blenheim.

1705 Sophia Charlotte, Queen of Prussia dies 1st February. Toland's *An Account of the Courts of Prussia and Hanover* published.

1707 Acts of Union or 'Union of the Crowns' uniting the kingdoms of England and Scotland.

1709 The Foreign and Protestants Naturalization Act 1709 passed by a Whig dominated parliament.
Toland's *Origines Judicae* published.

1712 Repeal of the Act of Naturalisation (1709).

A Letter against Popery by Sophia Charlotte of Prussia, (edited by Toland) published.

1713 Treaty of Utrecht.

1714 Sophia of Hanover dies 8th June.

Queen Anne dies August 1st, succeeded by George I.

Reasons for Naturalizing the Jews in Great Britain and Ireland is published in December.

Schism Act passed; later repealed by Religious Worship Act of 1718.

1715 Whigs take control of government in Britain beginning the period of "Whig Supremacy" (1715–60).

1718 *Nazarenus: or Jewish, Gentile, and Mahometan Christianity* published.

1722 Toland dies in London 11th March.

About this Book

This book is also available as a Kindle edition. Find it on Amazon.

Other Books by John Toland

An Account of the Courts of Prussia and Hanover;

Sent to a Minister of State in Holland (1705)

by John Toland

General Editor: J.N. Duggan

Published by **The Manuscript Publisher** (2013) and available in print and e-book editions. Further information about these and other titles is available from the websites of **The Manuscript Publisher** and **Books by J.N. Duggan**:

www.TheManuscriptPublisher.com/bookshop

and

BooksbyJNDuggan.com

Other Books to Read:

John Toland: Ireland's Forgotten Philosopher, Scholar …

and Heretic

by J.N. Duggan

Available in print and e-book editions. For further information please visit the websites of: TheManuscriptPublisher.com/bookshop and BooksbyJNDuggan.com

Also by J.N. Duggan

Sophia of Hanover: from Winter Princess to Heiress of Great Britain, 1630–1714

Published by Peter Owen Publishers, London, 2010

ISBN: 978 0 7206 1342 1

Available to Buy Online: www.BooksbyJNDuggan.com

Coming Soon:

Hans Axel Fersen: portrait of a gentleman

Publication Date: spring 2014

Made in the USA
Monee, IL
05 November 2026

67380483R00042